My

Dying Star

**True stories of impossible loves, of shadows,
departures… and hope.**

Author:
Smaille Eugène

Foreword

This book is a blend of life fragments.
Some of these stories are mine. Others belong to people
I've met, listened to, or simply walked with for a while. But
they all have something in common: they're true.

I didn't write these pages to teach anything, and certainly
not to present myself as an example. I wrote them to give
shape to what so many carry in silence. Because love, no
matter how beautiful, can also wound. It can shake us,
unroot us, or leave behind marks no one sees. This book is
about those kinds of love—the ones we romanticize, the
ones we miss, the ones we destroy without meaning to. But
also the ones that, even in pain, help us become who we
are.

I believe many will recognize themselves here. Maybe not
in every story. But perhaps in a sentence, a sensation, a
moment that echoes something from their own journey.
This book is for those who loved too much, too little, or
simply at the wrong time. For those who had to leave
despite the bond. For those who stayed despite the ache.
For those trying to make sense of what they lived, and for

those learning to love again—with more awareness, more softness, more maturity.

Each chapter speaks of a different kind of love. Some are destructive. Some are quiet. Some never had the chance to be lived fully. But through each story, you'll see the path of a heart that has learned—often the hard way—and that today wants to love differently.

If you're reading this, maybe there's still something inside you that hasn't found the right words yet. I hope these ones help. This isn't a guide. It's not a formula. Just a hand extended through memory, emotion, and all the truths we're often afraid to say out loud.

These pages aren't perfect.
But they're sincere.

— Me

Table of Contents

General Introduction

There are stories we only live once.
And then, there are those we never get to live at all—
yet they live inside us forever.

This book was born from those absences.
Not the kind we forget,
but the kind we carry.
The kind that doesn't scream,
but echoes softly in the background.
The kind with no clear ending,
yet a lingering taste of the unfinished.

We grow up believing love is supposed to be pure, mutual,
obvious.
That when it's right, it flows easily, without struggle.
But reality doesn't follow the same rules.

There are loves we never dared to name.
Loves we let slip away without knowing how to hold on.
Some that broke us.
Some that quietly built us—
even if they never fully took shape.

This book isn't a declaration.

It's not a reckoning.

It's a crossing.

A passage through the emotions we hide,

the scars we try to cover,

the memories we no longer know where to place.

The letters you're about to read are inspired by invisible

truths—

the kind that live in glances quickly turned away,

in words left unsaid,

in quiet longing,

in honest escape.

You won't find perfect love stories here.

But maybe, in the spaces between these lines,

you'll find parts of yourself.

Moments when you loved too hard.

When you waited.

When you tried and failed.

When you couldn't stay,

or couldn't leave.

These aren't heroic stories.
But they're deeply human.

This book is for those who couldn't quite say what they
felt.
For those who loved without return,
or walked away even when it hurt.
For those who rebuilt themselves quietly,
or loved too soon,
too badly,
too deeply.

If you feel a little lost here,
it's because you've already been here.
And if you recognize yourself,
know this:
you're not alone.

Sometimes, just putting things into words
makes the weight a little lighter.

This book is for you—
the one who reads,
the one who feels,
the one who's still healing.

Chapter Overview

This book explores different forms of love through fourteen initial stories, followed by seven more.
Each chapter dives into a unique emotional experience, marked by intensity, imbalance, lack, or inner transformation.
None of these loves are quite the same—
but they all leave a mark.

- **Chapter I – Exile**
  The one we love but cannot keep. Love made impossible by circumstances, distance, or life choices.

- **Chapter II – Fracture**
  The one that leaves a bitter taste. When trust is broken and love becomes a source of pain.

- **Chapter III – Too Soon**
  A love born too early, between two hearts too immature, not yet ready to love healthily.

believing in healing, but slowly fading under the weight of repetition and illusion.

- **Chapter X – Loving Silence**
  When everything is felt, but nothing is said. Hidden love, lived entirely on the inside.

- **Chapter XI – The Exchange**
  When one is replaced—not by a better love, but by a more convenient situation.

- **Chapter XII – Too Late, Too Right**
  When feelings are mutual, but life's timing is not.

- **Chapter XIII – Broken Mirror**
  A love that reflects us and forces us to face ourselves—for better or worse.

- **Chapter XIV – Holding Back**
  When we love, but hold back out of respect for someone else, or for a situation beyond our control.

- **Chapter XXI – Ready for Her**

  An open letter to the one to come, the one I finally feel ready for. The one I will love differently, consciously, with all the lessons of my past mistakes.

Love takes a thousand forms, but it always transforms us.

It never leaves us unscathed.

These are the stories of a man who loved the wrong way
too early,
too deeply,
or not enough.

But always sincerely.

What I've learned,
I've written.

What I've lost,
I've entrusted to these letters.

Chapter I — Exile

"There are bodies we leave behind, and souls we inhabit forever."

I left.
The world was calling,
life pulled me far from the arms that once knew how to calm me.
And you, you stayed.
On that land I walked away from,
with eyes still searching for me
even as my footsteps had already chosen exile.

You didn't scream.
Neither did I.
But in the silence between us
lay all the words we never found the courage to speak.

I remember your scent.
It clings to my memories like salt on the wind.
I remember your voice,
your silences full of questions I never knew how to answer.

And now, there is the ocean.

An ocean between your hand and mine.

Between your laughter and my nights.

Between our love and what life now demands of me.

You're still there,

but on the other side of the world.

You live, you breathe, you keep going—

and I wait for you without really waiting.

Every day I wonder:

Do you write to me in your mind?

Do you watch the moon, hoping we're looking at it

together?

Did you keep my voice tucked somewhere in your memory,

in that warm corner where some things still live?

I don't know.

But I kept you.

Not like something you cling to,

but like a soft light you let drift in your heart.

I write to you without sending it,

like writing to a falling star that's already disappeared from

view.

I love you in silence,

like a quiet song kept for oneself

when the world is too loud.

I wish time had waited for us.

That airplanes could be bridges, not farewells.

That borders were gentle,

and visas didn't separate souls.

But that's not how this story is written.

You are far, but you are here.

I ask your forgiveness.

Forgive me for leaving.

Forgive me for the emptiness I left behind.

Forgive me for not knowing exactly where we're going.

But I promise you one thing: I never played.

Not with you. Never.

You are my star.

The one I watch from afar,

but love up close.

The one I speak to in silence,

every night before I close my eyes.

And now...
I live with your memory
like a quiet fire burning in my chest.

You taught me that love is not always enough—
that sometimes leaving
is loving in silence.
And that some absences
are secret forms of presence.

May life be gentle with you,
my star who stayed behind
on that land I left—
a land that, because of you,
never really left me.

— Me

Chapter II — Fracture

"Some hands can caress and destroy at once. And some hearts still bleed for those."

Letter to my fallen star, the one I loved too fiercely

I don't know if I'm writing this letter for you... or for me.
I think it's a bit of both.
Because there's still a trace of you in my voice when I
speak softly,
in my silence when I remember,
in the nights where I search for answers.

You betrayed me.
But I won't begin this letter with anger.
I'll begin with a memory.

The memory of your smile,
of your hands that sometimes trembled when you said you
loved me.
I'll begin with tenderness,
because despite everything, I loved you with the heart of a
man who wanted to build.

You had that way of walking into my life like warm sunlight,
and leaving like a cold gust of wind.

I didn't see it coming.
Or maybe... I closed my eyes,
because love made me blind,
and I wanted to believe in you more than in my own doubts.

You didn't just share my everyday life.
You carried my dreams.
You held pieces of me I never gave to anyone else.

And yet,
you chose another voice,
another skin,
another laugh to drown in.

I felt empty.
Small.
Betrayed.

But even then, in the pain that folded my heart in two,
I never managed to hate you.

I ask your forgiveness.

Yes, forgiveness.

Not because I was guilty,

but because maybe I erased myself too much trying to keep you.

Because I loved too much—

so much that I forgot myself.

And no one should love to the point of forgetting who they are.

You left.

You destroyed what we were building.

But you also left behind something beautiful in my past.

And it's that trace I choose to keep.

Not your betrayal.

Not your escape.

But the real moments, the honest glances—

what truly existed… before it all collapsed.

Today, I no longer wait for you.

I don't search for you in others.

I live.

With this scar.

And with the tenderness still intact in me for you,

despite it all.

Safe travels, you who broke me.

I hold no grudge.

But I won't come back.

— Me

Chapter III — Too Soon

"Some loves lacked nothing but timing."

Letter to my star I met too soon

I think of you often...
Not with pain, but with that bittersweet sigh we breathe
when we remember a dream we never quite managed to
live through.

You were beautiful—
not just the kind of beauty one sees,
but the kind of presence that soothes,
the kind of voice that quiets our storms.

And I...
I was a man in disarray.
A man with suitcases full of unresolved stories,
and too many silences left in disarray.

I was there, but not really.
Present, but drifting.
Loving, but unable to love the way you deserved.

I ask your forgiveness.
Not just for leaving,
but for staying so long only halfway.

You deserved a whole love, a ready heart—
and I was still trying to piece mine back together.

You weren't the problem.
You were the gift that arrived too early,
into the hands of a man who hadn't yet stopped trembling.

I loved you.
I loved you clumsily and quietly,
like a boy discovering water but too afraid to dive in.

You weren't a passing moment.
You were a promise I failed to keep.

And every time I think of you,
I wonder what we might have become
if life had given us more time—
if I had known how to stay,
or if you had come just a little later,
when I had finally learned not to run from the things that
make the heart beat too hard.

Today, I move forward.
But I keep you, tucked away in a quiet corner of my memory.

Sometimes I send you silent thoughts—
not so you'll come back,
but so you'll know I haven't forgotten.

That even if I left,
I never stopped carrying you with me… gently.

If one day we meet again,
I don't know what we'll become.
But I know I'll look at you with gratitude,
and an infinite respect for the person you were in my life.

Thank you for believing in me,
even when I couldn't believe in myself.

And I'm sorry.
For leaving...
when I should have learned how to stay.

— Me

Chapter IV — Alone Together

"Some hearts give without limit, and end up drained in the silence of those who never knew how to receive."

Letter to my star, too full of me

You know,

I never knew how to love halfway.

I don't know how to pretend, or ration the intensity.

When I love, I give.

When I choose, I forget myself.

And with you… I forgot myself.

You were that waking dream holding my hand.

I needed nothing else.

I memorized the paths of your smile,

gave without counting,

loved you with the faith of a man who thought love would

be enough.

But love isn't enough when it travels alone.

I loved for two,

built a bridge between your silence and my hope,

and waited on the edge for you to cross it.

You never did.

Maybe you didn't want to.

Or maybe you couldn't.

And I don't blame you.

I write this without bitterness.

You didn't lie to me—you just let me believe.

And it was me, only me,

who refused to see that you weren't there the way I was.

I remember your absences even when you were right next
to me.

Your gaze wandering elsewhere,

your answers mechanical,

your tenderness reduced to politeness.

And me, in all of this—

I was that heart too full,

too much love in a world that prefers balance over excess.

I ask your forgiveness…

not for loving you too much,

but for losing myself in you.
I emptied myself trying to fill you,
exhausted myself waiting for an echo.

And when you left,
I didn't scream.
I collapsed in silence,
with that strange feeling of not knowing where I begin
anymore.

But I'm healing.
Slowly.
I'm learning to keep some love for myself,
to stop dissolving in others.

You taught me that love, to be beautiful,
must come back to you too.

And even if I loved alone,
even if you left,
I thank you for having existed in my world—
if only to remind me that I'm capable of loving fully,
even when it's too much.

So go…
and if one day you remember me,

remember the one who loved you like a refuge.

Excessively, maybe—

but always truthfully.

— Me

Chapter V — Nipped in the bud

"Not all breakups slam the door. Sometimes, we just quietly fade… in mutual indifference."

Letter to my star gone distant

You're still out there, somewhere.
And yet, it feels like you no longer exist.
We didn't really break up.
There was no end.
Just a slow fading…
Like a photo losing its color,
like a song we used to love but stopped playing,
for no particular reason.

I remember our laughter, our long late-night talks.
The words that flowed effortlessly,
that feeling of being understood before even speaking.

But now,
I reread our old messages like you read an old novel—
with nostalgia, and a hint of pain.

You don't write anymore.
Neither do I.
Not out of pride.
But because I no longer know what to say.
And maybe you don't either.

We became strangers in a world we once built together.
Two familiar bodies,
two silent hearts.

I still feel your name in my fingers,
but it slips like sand.

I don't know when it happened.
Maybe when the replies grew shorter.
Maybe when our "I'm thinking of you" disappeared.
Or maybe when we got used to the absence...
like we get used to an empty space.

And you know...
I do resent you a little.
Not for leaving.
But for staying without being there.
For fading away quietly, without a word—
as if I had never mattered.

And I ask forgiveness too.

For my silence,

for my own absences,

for the quiet expectations I never voiced.

I wanted you to fight a little,

to knock on my door,

to ask questions…

But you said nothing.

And I understood.

So now,

I keep what's left of you:

A few soft memories,

a pinch in the heart,

and this silence that's become normal.

Still, thank you.

For being there,

for a while.

And if our paths ever cross again,

I won't look away.

I'll look at you the way we look at a ghost we once loved—

with tenderness,

and without regret.

— Me

Chapter VI — Heavy to Carry

"Some people don't love your heart, but they love the warmth inside it."

My star

You never loved me.
And yet, you never wanted me to leave.

Because somehow, you loved the way I loved you.
You saw yourself reflected in the way I looked at you—
and that reflection made you feel beautiful,
unique, essential…
Even if, deep down, you didn't feel the same.

You didn't want commitment.
But you didn't want the emptiness my absence would leave
either.
So you stayed… halfway.
Close enough to be desired,
but distant enough to never truly love.

For a long time, I believed you were afraid.

Afraid to love, afraid to lose yourself, afraid of a past left unresolved.

But now I understand:

You didn't love me.

You loved being loved.

And I was good at it. Too good, maybe.

You fed on my tenderness,

on my quiet devotion,

on that unconditional loyalty I offered freely.

You didn't kiss me,

but you wouldn't let me breathe either.

You never said "stay,"

but did everything to make sure I'd never really go.

And I stayed.

Like a fire no one tends to,

but no one lets die.

I burned slowly, loving you in silence,

waiting for a sign… that would never come.

I gave you too much.

And you took it all,

without ever giving anything back.

Not out of cruelty,

but because my love was enough for you.

It was enough to fill a void I didn't create,

but that I kept feeding without realizing it.

Today, I'm leaving.

Not because I don't love you anymore,

but because I love myself a little more.

I no longer want to be a temporary shelter,

a heart visited only when yours feels too cold.

You taught me one thing:

It's not enough to be loved as we deserve.

We must also be loved by someone who knows how to
love.

And that wasn't you.

— Me

Chapter VII — The farewell that protects

"It's not that you don't want to love, it's that you haven't yet learned how to love without hurting the other."

Letter to the one who deserved a man ready

My star,

You may never truly understand why I left.

And maybe it's better that way.

Sometimes silence protects more than it wounds.

I loved you. God, how I loved you.

But I was a half-built man,

a heart under construction,

a mind still wrestling with its shadows.

I loved you with everything I had...

But what I had wasn't enough yet.

You were gentle, steady, clear.

I was fire, chaos, fragments.

I saw myself disappointing you with my silences,

hurting you without meaning to,

losing you slowly without the courage to shield you from it.

So I chose to leave.

Not because I didn't love you anymore,

but because I was too afraid I'd end up damaging you.

You deserved someone solid,

not a man still chasing his own answers.

You deserved steady arms, a reassuring gaze,

not this heart full of war, fighting not to hurt you.

I remember that last night.

Your eyes full of confusion,

my trembling hands,

and a kiss that lingered too long.

I wanted it to be gentle, even if it was the end.

I wanted you to remember me as someone brave enough to disappear.

I loved you like a lucid madman.

And everything I couldn't give you then,

I've built since, in my silences.

You'll never see it.

But know this: you were the spark that began my
reconstruction.

I won't come back.

It's not a promise—

it's a truth.

I write to tell you I'm sorry,

and that I hope the next one loves you with whole arms,

not stitched-up pieces of soul.

Thank you for believing in me.

Thank you for loving me, even when I didn't deserve it.

You were my light—

in a time when I didn't yet know how to walk toward it.

— **Me**

Chapter VIII — Gentle Blade

"Some hearts frighten—not because they hurt, but because they love too deeply."

Letter to the one I loved too much

My star,

I loved you like you love when you think it's the last time.

With that panicked fear of losing you,

with that desperate need to show you every day how much you mattered.

I didn't hold back.

I gave myself entirely.

And maybe that's where I went wrong.

You wanted space—

I gave you arms.

You wanted silence—

I wrote you poems.

You wanted time—

I offered you my nights.

I thought loving meant giving without condition.
I believed my devotion would make you feel special.

But by giving everything, I forgot how to breathe.
And you—
you drowned in the overflow.

I never meant to smother you.
I only wanted to make you feel safe,
to cover you in gentleness,
to love you the way I wished I'd been loved.

But sometimes, loving intensely scares those
who haven't yet learned how to receive.

You left quietly,
like turning off a light so as not to wake the room.

And I stayed there,
wondering what I'd done wrong.

But maybe it wasn't me...
Maybe you just didn't know what to do
with a love that asked for nothing in return.

I'm sorry.

For being too much.

For being there too often.

For loving too big, too soon, too truly.

I regret nothing—

except perhaps giving you a love

you weren't ready to hold.

And I hope someday you'll understand

that it's not intensity that wounds,

but the absence of reciprocity.

I still love. Differently now.

More quietly. But you,

I haven't forgotten.

— Me

Chapter IX — Despite Everything

"There are wounds we forgive... but can no longer marry."

Letter to the one I still love, but not enough to call "my wife"

You cheated on me.
I knew.
I felt it long before I heard it.
And yet...
I stayed.

I could've slammed the door,
become the cliché of the wounded man
who disappears without a word.

But I loved you too much
to leave at the first blow of your mistake.

So I stayed.
Out of love,
out of weakness maybe,
but mostly out of hope.

I convinced myself
that true love
endures the imperfect.

And I forgave you.
Not half-heartedly.
Truly.

I fought my doubts,
swallowed my anger,
choked on the humiliation.

For you.
For us.

But you did it again.
And this time,
something in me broke more quietly—
but deeper.

You see,
the problem isn't that I don't love you anymore.
I still do.

But I can't love you the same way.

I can't picture a future

with someone whose steps have already wandered twice.

I don't want to live with a heart on high alert.

I don't want to watch you sleep

and wonder if you're dreaming of someone else.

I love you too much

to trap you in my doubts.

And I love myself enough

not to become the shadow of a man.

I ask your forgiveness…

Forgive me if you hoped I'd be stronger.

Forgive me if you think I'm abandoning you.

But to stay now

would be to abandon myself.

You were beautiful.

You were gentle.

You were the calm in my storms.

But you were also one trial too many.

So I'm leaving.

With dignity.

Without hatred.

But with a tenderness that says:

"I truly loved you.

And that is precisely why

I can no longer choose you."

— Me

Chapter X – Loving in Silence

"To love without saying it is to scream without a mouth."

Letter to the one I loved in silence

I loved you without saying a word,

in that quiet night where there was no more room for

speech.

My whole heart beat for you—

but my mouth remained sealed,

like a door too afraid to open.

I never dared tell you.

I feared rejection, feared shattering everything.

To love in silence is a gentle ache,

a hidden wound masked by indifference.

I learned to watch you without your knowing,

to breathe in your scent without being seen,

to love you from the shadows,

in that soft light where nothing is spoken.

Now, thinking back on you,

I realize there was never truly an ending—

only a slow fading,

a distance I chose to place between us.

Maybe I was afraid of the truth.

Afraid of what it might mean

if I confessed that buried love.

Maybe you wouldn't have understood it.

Or maybe…

you wouldn't have wanted to.

I ask your forgiveness.

Forgive me for loving you silently.

Forgive me for leaving that part of myself in the dark.

I never opened my heart.

I left you trapped inside a silence heavy with meaning.

And yet—

that silence was my scream.

It was all I knew how to give.

I didn't know how to break the chains of my fear.

I don't want to keep you locked away in that silence

forever.

I just want you to know: I loved you.

With no conditions, no expectations,

only everything I had to offer.

And if you never knew…

I'm sorry.

Forgive me.

Maybe one day, in another life,

our words will finally meet.

And maybe then, the silence will break.

But until that day,

I'll keep your memory

in that secret corner of my heart—

the one where I never stopped loving you,

in silence.

—Me

Chapter XI – The Trade

"Some choices don't break the heart... they wake it."

Letter to the star who chose gold over love

I watched you leave.
Not like one watches a falling star—
but like watching a truth plummet
from a sky you still believed was blue.

You compared me.
Weighed me.
Measured me.
And found me lacking.

You didn't say it gently.
You threw it at me—
cold, raw,
like a slap to a man who still had hope.

He has money.
I had a heart.

And in your world,

riches bring more warmth than the arms of a sincere man.

You didn't choose "someone else."

You chose what he had.

And for that,

you walked all over me,

belittled me,

as if loving without wealth were a crime,

as if feelings were worth less than a bank account.

But I don't hate you.

I can't hate someone who simply doesn't know

how to love the way I do.

I don't hate you—

because I truly loved you.

And maybe that's what hurts most.

You were the woman I would've protected from

everything,

everything but her own emptiness.

You were my "maybe,"

my "what if,"

my "let's see."
But you became my "never."

I'm not angry.
I'm just… sad.
Sad that you believed love could be bought.
Sad that you looked at me with contempt,
when I would have given you the little I had
just to lift you up.

I'll never be rich like him.
But I would have been rich with you.
And that—
that wasn't enough for you.

So I'm leaving.
Not because I wasn't enough.
But because you wanted too little.

I'm sorry
for offering you a simple love
in a world that demands more.

I'm sorry
for not knowing how to shine any way
but through my heart.

And most of all—

thank you.

Thank you for showing me

that I deserve to be loved

without condition,

without scale,

without calculation.

I'll leave you with your other half.

And I'll take back mine—

bruised,

but whole.

—Me

Chapter XII – Too Late, Too Right

"Every time we found each other, it was already too late

for one of us."

Letter to you, the eternal almost

We crossed paths our whole lives.

At the wrong times.

In bodies too young or just ripe enough.

On familiar streets, or through unlikely chance.

You were always there—

at the wrong moment.

Or maybe it was me.

When I was ready to love,

you were crawling out of heartbreak.

When you were open to joy,

I was still clinging to ruins.

Every reunion felt like a missed miracle.
As if fate kept offering us a chance—
but always just one step off beat.

I remember the polite smiles.
The "it's been a while"
that hid every "what if."

I remember your scent
lingering on my sweater
as I walked home alone—again.

And I remember my dreams,
where our lives finally aligned—
but always, upon waking,
you vanished.

We never kissed.
Not really.
But I swear to you—
my soul kissed yours a thousand times.

You were my quietest fantasy,
my gentlest regret.
Not a sharp pain.
No.

A peaceful ache.
Like a song you never finish—
afraid you'll ruin the magic.

I'm sorry.
Sorry for the times I left too soon,
or stayed too long.

Sorry for thinking we'd always find our way back.

We never had the right timing.

But in another life,

I'll love you the second I see you.

And I'll say it without waiting.

—Me

Chapter XIII – Shattered Mirror

"We loved each other like two fires burning each other

down."

Letter to my reflection, distorted by love

You were me.
In the way you spoke, the way you thought, the way you
ran.
In your wounds that never fully healed,
in that gentle rage you hid behind your smile.
You were the mirror you stare into too long
until it finally swallows you whole.

I loved you the way one loves a forbidden truth—
with fascination, with fear.
I recognized you before I even knew your name,
as if our souls had already met
somewhere in an older pain.

Everything was fluid—
perhaps too fluid.

We anticipated each other's silences,
we understood our fears before they were spoken.
And it was beautiful...
until it burned.

We consumed ourselves trying to understand each other,
trying to heal in the other what we refused to face in
ourselves.
We were too alike.
Two hearts too sensitive,
too lucid,
too broken.

I loved you—
but sometimes, loving you felt like facing all the parts of
myself I couldn't stand.
And I know it was the same for you.
We saw each other too clearly.
We looked without filters.
Without lies.
And maybe that's why we destroyed each other.

I don't blame you.
I blame myself just as much.
But I owe you an apology.

I'm sorry I couldn't love your reflection
without casting my shadows onto it.
Sorry for making you pay for my storms.
Sorry for loving a version of myself through you,
instead of seeing you as you truly were.

You were me.
And I had to lose you
so I wouldn't completely lose myself.

— **Me**

Chapter XIV – Restraint

"Respect kept me away from you, even when everything

inside me screamed to stay."

Letter to the one I loved in silence, out of duty

You were there.
Within reach, soft, radiant.
And yet, I couldn't touch you.
Not because you were forbidden—
but because you were sacred.

I loved you.
With a quiet, deep, respectful love.
A love I tucked into the folds of my silence,
because looking at you
made me forget everything…
except my principles.

I loved you without saying a word,
out of loyalty to others,

to promises made,

to commitments that came before you.

I loved you without ever brushing against you,

never crossing that invisible line

where heart ends and duty begins.

And with every passing day, I died a little.

With every smile you gave me without knowing,

with every glance I turned away from,

afraid of losing my soul in your eyes.

I loved you unconditionally—

but under the weight of every condition in the world.

I don't know if you ever knew.

I don't know if you ever felt that stifled fire

in my restrained gestures,

in the tremble of my voice.

But I remember.

I remember everything I never said.

Everything I wanted to scream

but drowned in loyalty.

I'm sorry.

Sorry I never told you how much you meant to me.

Sorry I loved you in silence,

like a secret too pure to be touched by reality.

Sorry I didn't have the courage to choose love

and chose honor instead.

But know this—

I carried you inside me like a silent vow.

And even if the world will never know what we were,

I will.

Always.

— Me

Chapter XV – Hunger for You

"You loved me, but I loved you out of need, out of

emptiness, out of lack."

Letter to the one I loved out of dependency

My gentle star,
I write to tell you what often hides in silence.

The love I gave you was a muted cry,
a desperate plea echoing in the dark corners of my soul.
I loved you—
but not the way you deserved.

Because my love was laced with dependency,
a need that fed off your gestures, your words,
like a shelter I refused to leave,
even as it collapsed around me.

I didn't know how to love without needing.
Without that thirst burning from within.

I took without giving,

leaned on you to fill the cracks

that were never yours to mend.

I'm sorry.

Sorry I never gave you a free kind of love.

Sorry I made you believe

you were my lifeline,

when I was just a drowning man,

too weak to swim on his own.

You deserved lightness—

a love that didn't cling to you like a weight.

You deserved peace,

a love without chains,

one that didn't ask you to gather the broken pieces of my

heart.

But instead, I dragged you into my storm,

let you drown in my endless needs,

my insatiable demands,

my hollow expectations.

You loved me with all you had,

and I couldn't return that pure love.

Now I am alone with my flaws.

I can't come back to you.

I can't erase what's been done.

But know this—

everything you gave me,

I carry with me,

like a burning reminder of who I should have been.

This letter is not an excuse,

but a confession.

A way to say I'm sorry.

Sorry I loved you in a way that did you wrong.

Sorry I didn't know how to love

without depending on you.

You were the light in my darkness.

And I never gave you a clear sky.

Thank you for loving me,

even when you shouldn't have,

even when I was too selfish to see the beauty in your love.

I won't come back.

I won't return to the storm I created.

But even in my dependency,

you were my star.

And you taught me what love

was meant to be.

— Me

Chapter XVI – Poisoned Bond

"Toxic love is the kind where every word is a poison, and every gesture, poison in disguise."

Letter to the one I loved in a storm of destruction

My star,

I'm writing to you today with a clear mind, fully aware that

I was caught in a spiral of ruin—

a love where passion blurred into suffering,

where every touch carried the bitter taste of dependence,

and every burst of laughter hid a silent ache.

I loved you,

but that love was a poison swallowed in innocence,

believing each drop was necessary for survival,

when in truth, it was killing us softly, without warning.

We danced together,

but it was a dance on a razor's edge,

each step threatening to shatter our fragile balance.

I loved you, but I also destroyed—
as if my love had a shadow side,
a part that fed on the most delicate parts of us.

I asked too much of you.
I gave you too little.
And still, I waited for you to be everything.

And you,
you gave me the most precious parts of yourself,
but I let you pour them out
as if your love were an endless spring.

I'm sorry.
Sorry for making you believe that love could be fed by
pain,
sorry for weaving invisible chains between us—
chains you couldn't see,
but that tightened more each day.

I loved you with an obsession that suffocated you,
and I didn't even notice until it was far too late.

Some loves feel strong at first
because they burn so fiercely—

but they're just illusions,
cracks hidden behind forced smiles.

I'm sorry I didn't see those cracks.
Sorry I didn't step away before it all grew too heavy.

You deserved more than this chaos.
You deserved a love that didn't drain you,
that didn't leave you broken,
but one that filled you and helped you grow.

But I couldn't give you that kind of love.

I write this letter to say that I see it now—
that love is not supposed to be a war,
nor a prison.

Love is meant to be release.
A place where two souls meet and blossom,
not a place where they slowly destroy one another.

I'm sorry I made you believe you had to suffer in order to
love me.
You deserved a healthy love,
one that made you smile instead of cry.

I learned the hard way that toxic love scorches everything in its path.

And I'm truly sorry I was the one who burned through your beauty.

I won't come back.

But I hope you find a love that heals all the wounds I left behind—

a love that is free, steady, and nourishing.

Thank you for having been there.

And I'm deeply sorry for all I put you through.

— Me

Chapter XVII – What Remains

"Resilient love is the kind that rises from its ashes, ready to love again—even after being broken."

Letter to the one I loved through it all

My star,
I write to you after storms have passed,
after watching my heart shatter and piece itself back
together,
like a falling star breaking into light before it shines
again—
stronger, brighter, and more awake.

Our love was forged in hardship,
a love that didn't collapse at the first tremor,
but that sometimes sank to its knees,
tired, fragile,
yet still willing to rise.

I loved you in the pain,
but also in the healing.
Because every wound brought us closer,

and every obstacle taught us how to love
with more depth, more truth.

Resilient love is the kind that doesn't fade,
not even in the storm's eye.
It's the love that gets back up,
that finds the strength to forgive, to rebuild, to begin again.

We were broken—
but we knew how to mend.
And though the scars remain,
they are part of our story now.

I loved you with my weaknesses,
and you loved me with yours.
We learned to love within our imperfections,
to understand that love doesn't mean the absence of pain,
but the ability to hold each other when it arrives.

I'm sorry for the times I wasn't strong enough,
for the moments I almost let go.
But I know now—
true strength often hides in fragility.

We survived so much.
And somehow, I believe we learned to love harder, too.

You taught me resilience.

You showed me that real love isn't a destination,

but a path—twisted, yes, but always rich with meaning.

And even if that path led us apart,

what we lived mattered.

Deeply.

I regret nothing.

Every moment beside you made me grow,

taught me how to love differently—

with a depth I didn't know before.

And if one day our paths cross again,

it will be with a love that is steadier, wiser,

maybe even more resilient.

Thank you—

for your love,

your patience,

your strength.

You will remain in my heart,

no matter where life takes us.

— Me

Chapter XVIII – Gentle Erosion

"Some loves we embrace even knowing they'll never fully be ours... because the soul doesn't recognize status or timing."

Letter to the star I loved... even when she was never mine

You weren't free—
and I knew that.

You already had someone.
A man. A past. A promise.

And still,
I opened my door.
I let you in.
Or maybe I slipped quietly into your life
through a hidden door.

Not out of pride.
Not for the thrill.
But because, from the start,
I felt you—

real in your contradictions,

beautiful in your unease,

alive in your silences.

You never promised me the impossible.

You were honest, even in your confusion.

And I—

I accepted being the other shore,

the shelter,

the breath between obligations.

I knew you weren't mine.

And still,

every glance, every tremble, every shared moment

screamed that somewhere,

your heart beat louder with me.

But loving someone who belongs to another story

is like walking barefoot on glass.

Every moment is beautiful—

but it cuts.

I watched you leave,

after telling me how safe you felt,

how peaceful,

how with me, you could breathe again.

And still, you went back.

Not out of fear.

But loyalty.

Because you are that kind of woman—

faithful, even in the middle of the storm.

And I loved you.

Not like a thief of hearts,

but like a man who still hoped

love might one day open a door.

But yours stayed closed.

Not because you didn't love me,

but because you weren't ready

to destroy what you had already built.

So… I chose to leave.

Not from lack of love,

but because there was too much.

I loved you too much to watch you become

the one who hides,

who lies,

who suffers in silence

to keep up the illusion of a life built for two.

I loved you too much to remain the hidden chapter,

the man in the shadows.

I wanted to love you in the light.

But you couldn't.

I don't blame you.

I understand.

And I ask your forgiveness—

for taking your hand, knowing it wasn't free,

for leading you into a fire

while your heart was already bound elsewhere.

But thank you—

for sharing that flicker of light with me,

however brief,

for that forbidden tenderness,

for that unspoken truth that said:

"If the world were different, maybe we could have been
everything."

Today, I walk away—
not to forget,
but so you can keep looking at yourself in the mirror
without shame.

I leave to protect you—
from me, from yourself,
from what we might have become.

Because there are loves we leave
not out of weakness,
but out of respect.

— Me

Chapter XIX – Between Two Waves

"Love, at times, feels like a calm sea, then suddenly, a storm."

Letter to the one I loved through instability

My star,
Some loves don't know where they're going.
They rise and fall like tides,
shifting like a sea that never shows the same face twice.
I loved you in that ebb and flow,
never sure what would come next.

Your love, like mine,
was never steady.
Days of ecstasy, days of ache.
Silent promises, words left unsaid,
and always that push and pull,
leaving us suspended in midair.

There were moments when I believed everything was
perfect,
when your gaze found mine and the world held its breath.

And then suddenly, the distance would swell—

as if the sea turned wild—

and I'd be lost again,

drowning in the storm without understanding why.

To love like that is like trying to hold wind in your hands.

Every second was precious,

and every second made me wonder:

"Is what we have real, or just an illusion our hearts

created?"

I ask your forgiveness

if my own tides added to your confusion.

Forgive me for being there,

then suddenly not,

when my heart was torn between what I wanted

and what I was truly able to give.

In that shifting sea, I learned

that love isn't always linear,

and sometimes it fluctuates—

not because it's less real,

but because we, as humans, are layered and tangled,

and what we feel today can shape-shift by tomorrow.

But it isn't the change in love I regret.

It's not having known how to navigate those waves more

wisely,

letting the storm carry me away.

I've learned that we need to be steadier,

quieter in the face of life's tides,

more constant when the heart trembles.

Thank you for every moment—

the highs and the lows—

because they helped me grow.

Thank you for being that wind, that motion,

that taught me not to fear instability,

but to find peace in still waters,

and to understand that love isn't something to control,

but to live fully, in all its beautiful, bewildering complexity.

— **Me**

Chapter XX – Human

"Love is never perfect. It's perfect because it isn't."

Letter to the one I loved through all our imperfections

My star,
There is no such thing as perfect love—
and yet, that's exactly what makes it so precious.

We were never perfect.
Never the flawless picture people dream of,
the kind they write into film scripts.
And that's what made our love real.

Every wrong word,
every clumsy gesture,
every shared misunderstanding—
everything that wasn't perfect
taught me how to love with my flaws and yours.

Because true love doesn't lie in seeking perfection,
but in learning to accept the other,
entirely,
in all their imperfect beauty.

I remember our endless fights,
the disagreements that pulled us apart,
only to bring us closer again.

It wasn't the beauty of the words or gestures
that made it special,
but those moments when—despite it all—
we chose to forgive,
to rediscover each other again and again,
despite the bruises.

I ask your forgiveness for the times I acted thoughtlessly,
for the moments I left you in doubt,
for when my words cut deeper than I meant.
Forgive me for everything I almost became,
and everything I wasn't enough of.

But because of you,
I've come to see that love needs no perfection—
only sincerity, acceptance and patience.

It's in our flaws, our hesitations,
our cracks and our scars
that love finds its light.

I don't regret anything we lived through,

not even our hardest moments,

because it was that very imperfection

that forged my heart taught me to love with all that I am,

even the parts of me I used to hide.

Thank you.

You showed me that love doesn't ask to be perfect,

only to be lived truthfully, tenderly, vulnerably.

And I am deeply grateful

to have lived all of that with you.

— **Me**

Chapter XXI – Ready for Her

*"I have loved, I have suffered, but now I am finally ready to
love you."*

You are here.

Or maybe not yet.

Maybe you're reading this in silence,

or waiting for me without even knowing it's me.

But one thing is certain:

I've carried you inside me long before we ever met.

I searched for you

in glances, in silences,

in the wounds I never wanted to reopen.

I loved poorly.

I loved too soon, too hard, too hollow.

And every fall taught me how to rise—

not to impress you...

but so that I wouldn't lose you

when I finally found you.

I'm no longer afraid to love.
I'm no longer afraid to be vulnerable,
to say: I need you.

But not because I'm incomplete.
No...
because I want us to choose each other freely,
every day,
without conditions or twisted expectations.

When you arrive—or if you're already here—
I want you to know this:

I won't come to you with empty promises.
I won't try to save you.
I won't love you to fill a void.

I will come whole,
clear-eyed,
present.

I'll be here to listen,
to hold space for your moods, your doubts, your past.
And I will offer you mine,
without masks, without retreat.

I don't expect you to be perfect.
I only ask that you be true.

I am no longer that man who ran away,
nor the broken heart that only loved halfway.
I've become someone who understands—
someone who knows that love
isn't about possession,
but construction—
built day by day, together.

So if you are here…
look at me.

I'm ready.
Not to impress you,
but to walk beside you.
Not to hold you down,
but to choose you.
Not to promise you a world without storms,
but to reach for your hand when everything shakes.

And if you ever read this one day,
know that this chapter
is the door I leave open for you.

There's no need to knock.
Come in.

— Me, today

Conclusion

Love, like a river that twists and turns without warning, has often slipped through my fingers. At times, it broke me—leaving behind wounds I took years to understand. But it also taught me. It showed me that pain is not an ending, but a path—a way to be reborn, to become something new.

This book is not a revenge on heartbreak, nor a way to dwell on the past. It is not an attempt to fix what was broken, nor a desperate cry to recover what might have been. This book is an offering. An offering of words to soothe the souls who, like mine, have learned to love in incompletion—to love despite the cracks.

It is not a book of easy comforts, but a mirror held up to those who, one day, loved without return, loved too fiercely, or too late. To you, reading these lines—maybe you saw yourself in a chapter, a sentence, a silence. Maybe you've felt that same ache, that same hesitation, that same search for meaning. Know this: you were never alone. Behind every story here is a heart that once bled, but after rising again, learned to beat differently.

I have not become perfect. I still carry fractures, unhealed wounds, painful memories. But I've learned one essential truth: love is not enough unless it is free, clear-eyed, and gentle. It is not enough to love—we must learn how to love well, with responsibility, with kindness, and with the ability to see the other as they are, not as we wish them to be.

I hope that somewhere, these words have brought you a measure of peace. And if, one day, you meet someone you truly love—do not wait to lose them before you understand their worth. Love them now. Love them in the way you wish you had been loved. Love them with your flaws, your strengths—but most of all, love them well. And don't forget to love yourself. For without that love, nothing else is truly possible.

Love begins within—so it can shine outward toward those we hold close.

Acknowledgments

I want to express my gratitude to everyone who crossed my path and left a mark. Thank you to those who hurt me—whether knowingly or not. You taught me to strengthen my heart, to understand that pain is part of life, but it is not the end. It is a transition.

Thank you to those who loved me, even when I didn't feel worthy of that love. You showed me the beauty of unconditional acceptance—the importance of love without expectations, without limits. Through you, I learned that pure love asks for nothing in return, only that it be lived, fully.

Thank you to those who left without explanation. Sometimes, silence speaks louder than a thousand words. And to those who stayed despite my silences, despite my doubts, despite my wounds—you saw beyond what I allowed the world to see. You taught me patience, perseverance, and the quiet art of staying, even when leaving seemed easier.

This book exists because of you. It exists because of your gestures, your silences, your presence, and your absence.

You have nourished these pages with your stories, your heartbreak, and your healing. And to all those who shared their story with me—or whose silences inspired my words—you have been an endless well of inspiration.

I owe you this truth: love, in all its forms, is an infinite wealth, a never-ending source of growth.

Author's Note

Some of the stories you've read in these chapters are deeply personal. They come from my own experiences, my wanderings, my wounds. Others, however, are drawn from those around me—people who have shared their truths with me. But all of these stories are real. They are as authentic as the emotions that accompany them, whether joyful, painful, or resigned.

If you saw yourself in these pages, perhaps it's because love, in its fractures and unfulfilled desires, makes us all alike. We're not so different in the way we love, wait, long, and suffer. We all have a heart that beats for someone, even if sometimes that heart follows a path parallel to another, never quite crossing.

I am neither a moralist nor a guide. I don't pretend to hold the ultimate truth about love. What I do know is that I chose to put words to my pain, my forgiveness, my letting go. I chose to share what shaped me, what broke me, and ultimately, what taught me to love differently.

My sincerest hope is that these words brought you some comfort, clarity, or understanding. Perhaps one day you'll look back on this reading and say, "I understood something more about myself, about love, about those I once loved." And if that happens, then I'll know I've fulfilled my purpose.

Thank you for taking this journey with me.

Final Words

To the one who is here—or who may come later... I hope
to love you without fear. I hope not to repeat my mistakes.
And if you read this book one day, whether you're by my
side or not, know that you are the answer to all my
unfinished questions.

Based on true stories

A book for those who have loved... and survived